First edition for the United States, Canada and
the Philippines published 1993 by Barron's Educational Series, Inc.
Text copyright © Debbie MacKinnon 1993
Illustrations copyright © Anthea Sieveking 1993

Conceived and produced by Frances Lincoln Limited
Apollo Works, 5 Charlton Kings Road, London NW5 2SB

All inquiries should be addressed to:
Barron's Educational Series, Inc.
250 Wireless Boulevard
Hauppauge, NY 11788

Library of Congress Catalog Card No. 92-21830
International Standard Book No. 0-8120-6334-1

Library of Congress Cataloging-in-Publication Data
MacKinnon, Debbie
  Baby's first year / Debbie MacKinnon: photographs by Anthea
Sieveking — 1st ed.
  Summary: Photographs and brief text describes a baby's growth and
development from one day to one year old.
  ISBN 0-8120-6334-1
  1. Infants—Juvenile literature. 2. Infants—Development—
—Juvenile literature. [1. Babies.] I. Sieveking, Anthea, ill.
II. Title.
HQ774. M23 1993
305.23′2—dc20   92-21830

Printed and bound in Hong Kong

3456   987654321

Baby's first year

Debbie MacKinnon

Photographs by Anthea Sieveking

BARRON'S

One day old

Happy Birthday, Neil!
Welcome to the world.
Neil is crying because
everything seems new
and strange.

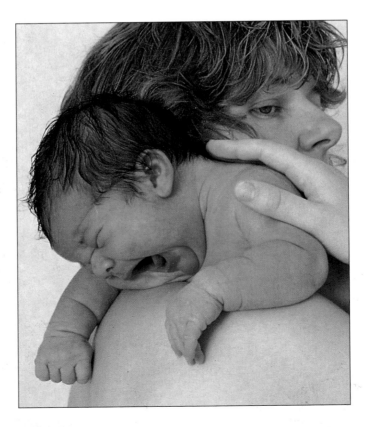

One week

Neil drinks milk from his Mommy.

Then he brings up a burp.

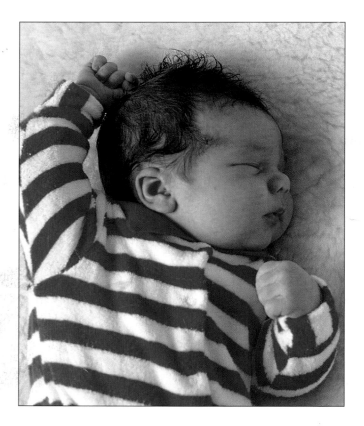

But he spends most of the time fast asleep!

When Neil wakes up, he needs to be washed and changed. His big sisters, Susan and Debbie, like to help.

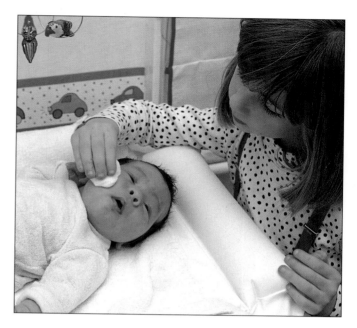

Easy does it!

Six weeks

Neil makes lots of funny faces…

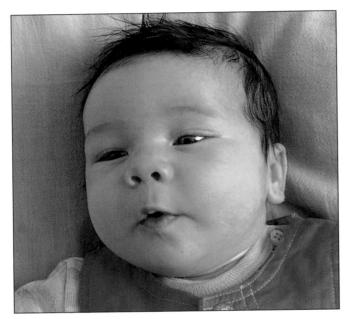

Oooooh!

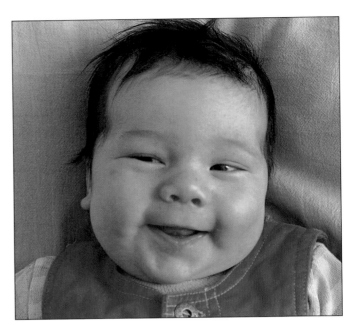

What a big smile!

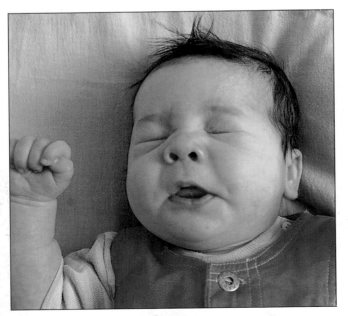

Aa-kerchoo!

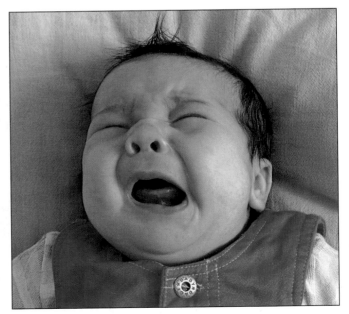

Waaaah!

Three months

Neil is starting to use his hands.

 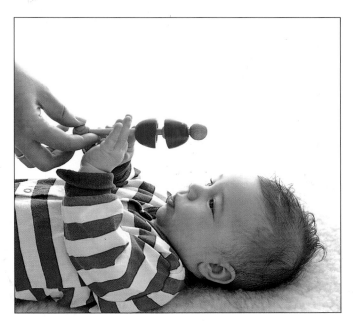

He can touch a toy and he tries to hold one.

But his best toys   are his own fingers.

Four months

Time to get up!
Daddy plays peek-a-boo
with Neil, while he gets dressed.

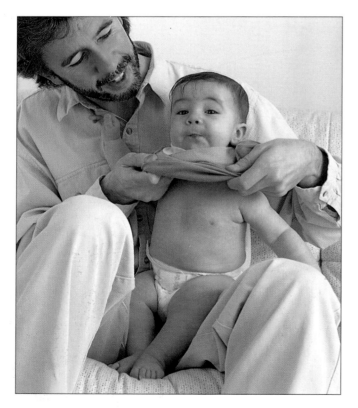

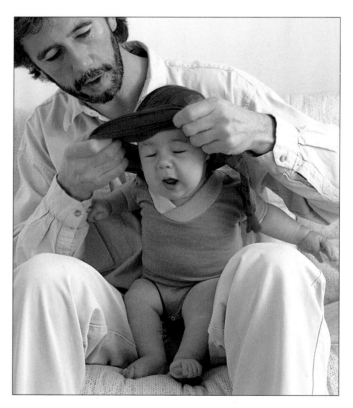

Pull on the vest.
Peek-a-boo!

Where is Neil?
Peek-a-boo!

 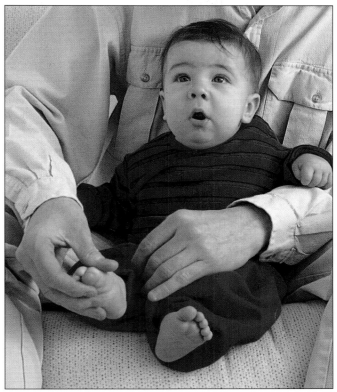

Where are your toes? This little piggy...

All ready for a tickle!

Five months

Now Neil enjoys going out to see the world. Sometimes he goes in the car, sometimes he rides in the buggy, but best of all he loves the back pack.

Straps on!

Off we go!

Hold on tight!

Six months

Neil can move around
by rolling over...

...and over on
the floor.

He thinks he is very clever!

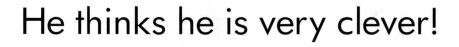

Seven months

Neil can sit up
all by himself.
Can you see his
two new teeth?

He loves to look
at books.

Come on Neil,
push up...

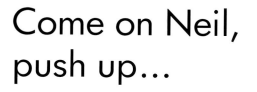

nearly crawling...

that's better...

Whoops!
down again!

Eight months

Neil is eating bread and carrot while he waits for his lunch.

Open wide!

Neil can use a spoon...

but fingers are easier!

All gone!

Neil can crawl, but he wants to stand. He pulls himself up by holding onto Susan. The girls are teaching Neil to talk. "Ball," they say. "Ba-ba-boo," says Neil.

Neil has a splash with
his sisters to cool off.

But he makes a big fuss
when it's time to get out!

Ten months

It's bathtime! Neil is crawling, so he gets very dirty! He wants to stand up while Mommy takes his clothes off. No! Don't touch, Neil.

Can you catch the water, Neil?

What a dirty face!

Hello, hello…is anyone there?

Time to get out. Don't cry, Neil.

Look, Neil can brush his teeth. Very good!

Eleven months

Neil is ready to take his first steps. Let go of Daddy's legs, Neil! "Dada," says Neil as he wobbles over to Daddy, holding out his arms.

Two weeks later Neil is walking well by himself. He can even bend down to get his toy duck without falling over.

Twelve months

Happy Birthday, Neil!
One year old today —
What a big boy you are!

First times...

First cry.

First smile.

First solid food.

First time sitting up.

First crawl.

First teeth.

First word — "Dada." First steps!